Forrester

by Iain Gray

Lang Syne

PUBLISHING

WRITING *to* REMEMBER

LangSyne
PUBLISHING
WRITING *to* REMEMBER

79 Main Street, Newtongrange,
Midlothian EH22 4NA
Tel: 0131 344 0414   Fax: 0845 075 6085
E-mail: info@lang-syne.co.uk
www.langsyneshop.co.uk

Design by Dorothy Meikle
Printed by Ricoh Print Scotland
© Lang Syne Publishers Ltd 2014

All rights reserved. No part of this publication may be reproduced, stored
or introduced into a retrieval system, or transmitted in any form or by any
means (electronic, mechanical, photocopying, recording or otherwise) without
the prior written permission of Lang Syne Publishers Ltd.

ISBN 978-1-85217-464-4

Forrester

MOTTO:
Blaw hunter blaw thy horn
(Blow hunter, blow your horn).

CREST:
The head of a hound.

TERRITORY:
Edinburgh and Stirlingshire.

NAME variations include:
Forest
Forester
Forister
Forrest
Forrister
Forster
Foster

*The spirit of the clan means
much to thousands of people*

Chapter one:

The origins of the clan system

by Rennie McOwan

The original Scottish clans of the Highlands and the great families of the Lowlands and Borders were gatherings of families, relatives, allies and neighbours for mutual protection against rivals or invaders.

Scotland experienced invasion from the Vikings, the Romans and English armies from the south. The Norman invasion of what is now England also had an influence on land-holding in Scotland. Some of these invaders stayed on and in time became 'Scottish'.

The word clan derives from the Gaelic language term 'clann', meaning children, and it was first used many centuries ago as communities were formed around tribal lands in glens and mountain fastnesses.

The format of clans changed over the centuries, but at its best the chief and his family held the land on behalf of all, like trustees, and the ordinary clansmen and women believed they had a blood relationship with the founder of their clan.

There were two way duties and obligations. An inadequate chief could be deposed and replaced by someone of greater ability.

Clan people had an immense pride in race. Their relationship with the chief was like adult children to a father and they had a real dignity.

The concept of clanship is very old and a more feudal notion of authority gradually crept in.

Pictland, for instance, was divided into seven principalities ruled by feudal leaders who were the strongest and most charismatic leaders of their particular groups.

By the sixth century the 'British' kingdoms of Strathclyde, Lothian and Celtic Dalriada (Argyll) had emerged and Scotland, as one nation, began to take shape in the time of King Kenneth MacAlpin.

Some chiefs claimed descent from ancient kings which may not have been accurate in every case.

By the twelfth and thirteenth centuries the clans and families were more strongly brought under the central control of Scottish monarchs.

Lands were awarded and administered more and more under royal favour, yet the power of the area clan chiefs was still very great.

The long wars to ensure Scotland's

independence against the expansionist ideas of English monarchs extended the influence of some clans and reduced the lands of others.

Those who supported Scotland's greatest king, Robert the Bruce, were awarded the territories of the families who had opposed his claim to the Scottish throne.

In the Scottish Borders country – the notorious Debatable Lands – the great families built up a ferocious reputation for providing warlike men accustomed to raiding into England and occasionally fighting one another.

Chiefs had the power to dispense justice and to confiscate lands and clan warfare produced a society where martial virtues – courage, hardiness, tenacity – were greatly admired.

Gradually the relationship between the clans and the Crown became strained as Scottish monarchs became more orientated to life in the Lowlands and, on occasion, towards England.

The Highland clans spoke a different language, Gaelic, whereas the language of Lowland Scotland and the court was Scots and in more modern times, English.

Highlanders dressed differently, had different

customs, and their wild mountain land sometimes seemed almost foreign to people living in the Lowlands.

It must be emphasised that Gaelic culture was very rich and story-telling, poetry, piping, the clarsach (harp) and other music all flourished and were greatly respected.

Highland culture was different from other parts of Scotland but it was not inferior or less sophisticated.

Central Government, whether in London or Edinburgh, sometimes saw the Gaelic clans as a challenge to their authority and some sent expeditions into the Highlands and west to crush the power of the Lords of the Isles.

Nevertheless, when the eighteenth century Jacobite Risings came along the cause of the Stuarts was mainly supported by Highland clans.

The word Jacobite comes from the Latin for James – Jacobus. The Jacobites wanted to restore the exiled Stuarts to the throne of Britain.

The monarchies of Scotland and England became one in 1603 when King James VI of Scotland (1st of England) gained the English throne after Queen Elizabeth died.

The Union of Parliaments of Scotland and England, the Treaty of Union, took place in 1707.

Some Highland clans, of course, and Lowland families opposed the Jacobites and supported the incoming Hanoverians.

After the Jacobite cause finally went down at Culloden in 1746 a kind of ethnic cleansing took place. The power of the chiefs was curtailed. Tartan and the pipes were banned in law.

Many emigrated, some because they wanted to, some because they were evicted by force. In addition, many Highlanders left for the cities of the south to seek work.

Many of the clan lands became home to sheep and deer shooting estates.

But the warlike traditions of the clans and the great Lowland and Border families lived on, with their descendants fighting bravely for freedom in two world wars.

Remember the men from whence you came, says the Gaelic proverb, and to that could be added the role of many heroic women.

The spirit of the clan, of having roots, whether Highland or Lowland, means much to thousands of people.

*Clan warfare produced a society where courage
and tenacity were greatly admired*

Chapter two:

Ancient roots

Both a locational and an occupational surname, 'Forrester' originally denoted someone who lived in or near a forest, or worked in a forest.

Found from earliest times throughout the length and breadth of the present-day United Kingdom, it was particularly prevalent in the north of England and the Midlothian and Stirlingshire areas of the Scottish Lowlands.

One theory is that those Forresters of today of Scottish descent may boast ancient Celtic/Druidic roots through a descent from Marnin the Forester, who is known to have held lands in Dunipace, Stirlingshire, at the turn of the thirteenth century.

Whatever their origins, what is known with certainty is that it is from an early date that the Forresters began to appear in the historical record.

An Archebaldus Forrester is recorded in Lesmahagow, Lanarkshire, in 1164, while John le Forester, a Berwickshire landowner, appears in the infamous *Ragman Roll* of 1296.

Scotland had been thrown into crisis ten years

before this date, with the death of Alexander II and the death four years later of his successor, the Maid of Norway, who died while en route to Scotland to take up the crown.

John Balliol was enthroned at Scone as King of Scots in 1292 – but fatefully for the nation the ambitious Edward I of England had been invited to arbitrate in the bitter dispute over the succession to the throne, and the hapless Balliol was Edward's chosen man.

The Scots rose in revolt against the imperialist designs of the English king in July of 1296 but, living up to his reputation of 'Hammer of the Scots', he brought the entire nation under his subjugation little less than a month later, garrisoning strategic locations throughout the nation.

To reinforce his domination of Scotland, 1,500 earls, bishops, burgesses and other landowners were required to sign the humiliating treaty of fealty known as the *Ragman Roll*, because of the number of ribbons that dangled from the seals of the reluctant signatories.

It is on this document that the name of John le Forester is found – indicating that by this period he was judged as being in the higher ranks of Scottish society.

There are two main branches of the Forresters

in Scotland – Clan Forrester of Corstorphine, in Edinburgh, and the Forresters of Garden, in Stirlingshire.

Although considered today to be an armigerous clan, meaning that they now have no officially recognised Chief, for centuries the Chiefs of the Name were the Forresters of Corstorphine, where they held Corstorphine Castle.

The founder of the clan is recognised as Sir Adam Forrester – who was not only a merchant, provost of Edinburgh and ambassador, but also entrusted with the honoured post of Keeper of the Great Seal of Scotland.

His son, Sir John Forrester, was also honoured as Keeper of the Great Seal, in addition to Chamberlain of Scotland and Keeper of the Household of James I.

In 1633, Sir George Forrester, 10th Chief of Clan Forrester, was raised to the peerage as the 1st Lord of Corstorphine after being created a Baronet of Nova Scotia.

James VI first granted these baronetcies in 1624 to Scots of substance who were willing to invest in what was Scotland's first attempt to establish a colony in North America.

The area for proposed colonisation took in not only present-day Nova Scotia but also New Brunswick and the territory between there and the St Lawrence River.

Nearly forty Scottish magnates, initially, were granted allotments of territory and, although not physically required to take up possession of their distant new lands, a special ceremony was enacted on the Castle Hill of Edinburgh.

It was here that a small area was designated 'Nova Scotia' to allow them to formally take 'possession' of their land and be duly honoured with their baronetcy.

Nova Scotia, in effect, had been 'incorporated' into the Scottish kingdom, while the scheme marked the introduction of the honour of baronet to Scotland.

A combination of factors, including the terms of a peace treaty between England and France, led to the colony finally being abandoned in 1632.

The male line of the Forresters of Corstorphine eventually died out and passed through marriage through the female line to the Earls of Verulam.

The barony of Corstorphine finally passed out of Forrester hands in 1869 when it was sold to a John

Dickson, remaining in his family for more than 100 years until given to the Corstorphine Trust in 1986.

Nearly twenty years later, in 2005, the barony passed from the trust to Michael John Milne, entitling him to be recognised as 34th Baron of Corstorphine.

Although not officially recognised as such by the Lord Lyon King of Arms of Scotland – the ultimate authority on all matters pertaining to Scottish heraldry – the 'Chief' of Clan Forrester today is Sir John Duncan Grimston, 7th Earl of Verulam and 16th Lord Forrester of Corstorphine.

With his seat at Gorhamburg, in St Albans, Hertfordshire, he is the patron of the proud Clan Forrester Society.

Other cadet branches of the Forresters of Corstorphine are the Forresters of Niddry and the two French cadet branches of Le Forestier de Foucrainville, in Normandy, and Le Forestier du Buisson-Sainte-Marguerite, founded through descendants of Sir Adam Forrester.

The other main branch of Clan Forrester is the Forresters of Garden, Stirlingshire, who were hereditary keepers of what was the great royal forest and hunting ground of Torwood, near Bannockburn.

Rather intriguingly, part of Torwood once

held a sacred grove where the Celtic Druids carried out their mysterious ceremonies.

This may explain the tradition, noted above, that Forresters may have Celtic/Druidic links through Marnin the Forester.

Until the advent of the Hanoverian dynasty in the early eighteenth century, the Scottish monarchy was firmly rooted in ancient Celtic culture and tradition.

It was as part of this tradition, for example, that kings were enthroned at Scone on the Stone of Destiny, while a sennachie, or bard, would recite from memory a royal lineage stretching back into the past.

This Celtic tradition may also explain why Forresters had been entrusted as Keepers of the Great Seal – symbolic of the Community of the Realm of Scotland.

Not only custodians of Torwood, the Forresters of Garden also held other high royal positions – with Sir Duncan Forrester, for example, serving as Comptroller to the Royal Household of James IV.

The Forresters of Garden also gave rise to yet another cadet branch, the Forresters of Strathendry, near Leslie, Fife, builders of the sixteenth century Strathendry Castle.

Lasting legacies of both the Forresters of Garden and the Forresters of Corstorphine include the relic known as the Corstorphine Pendant, a magnificent armorial pendant of gilded bronze now on display in the Royal Museum of Scotland, Edinburgh.

Other precious heirlooms include the fifteenth century vellum book of Eastertide Music, *Sir Duncan Forrester's Antiphony*, in the Church of the Holy Rude, Stirling, where there is also the former private family chapel now known as the Forrester Aisle.

Yet another treasured relic is the Corstorphine Casket, made of carved oak and mounted in silver and thought to have been a gift from Margaret Tudor, wife of James IV, to Sir Duncan Forrester.

Chapter three:

On the field of battle

It was from the earliest times that Forresters were prominent on the field of battle, often at great cost to themselves, in defence of Scotland's freedom.

During the bloody Wars of Independence with England, bearers of the name fought at the side of Robert the Bruce and, in 1333, nineteen years after the great warrior king's victory at Bannockburn, they were among the ranks of Scots at the battle of Halidon Hill.

Fought in the summer of that year during the Second War of Scottish Independence, a force under the command of Sir Archibald Douglas was heavily defeated by an army of England's Edward III at Halidon Hill, about two miles north west of Berwick-upon-Tweed.

One contemporary account of the battle, contained in *The Lanercost Chronicle*, notes how the Scots were mown down in their scores as they attempted to ascend the hill in the face of heavy fire from arrows.

The chronicle states how:

The Scots who marched in the front were so

wounded in the face and blinded by the multitude of English arrows that they could not help themselves, and soon began to turn their faces away from the blows of the arrows and fall.

Nearly 70 years later, in 1402, Sir John Forrester, Keeper of the Great Seal of Scotland, fought at the side of James I at the battle of Homildon Hill, also known as Humbleton Hill, in Northumberland.

A 10,000-strong Scottish force under the command of the colourful Archibald Douglas, 4th Earl of Douglas, had crossed the border and laid waste most of the northern English area of Northumberland before suffering a decisive defeat – common with the battle of Halidon Hill, largely as a result of the deadly firepower of the skilled English and Welsh archers.

In June of 1488 the Forresters fought in support of the beleaguered James III at the battle of Sauchieburn, about two miles south of Stirling and close to the site of the 1314 battle of Bannockburn.

It was here that a 30,000-strong force loyal to James gave battle to an 18,000-strong force led by a number of powerful and dissident nobles who aimed to put the king's 15-year-old heir, Prince James, Duke of Rothesay, on the throne.

The battle proved inclusive, but the rebels

won the day when James was killed, under mysterious circumstances, after fleeing the battlefield.

One account of his death is that he was killed after being thrown from his horse, while another is that he was stabbed to death by a rebel dressed as a priest.

Whatever the circumstances of his death, his son, who indeed succeeded his father to the throne as James IV, afterwards constantly wore a heavy iron chain around his waist as a decidedly uncomfortable reminder of his role in his father's death.

In September of 1513, Sir John Forrester of Niddry and Sir David Forrester of Torwood were among the 5,000 Scots – including James IV, an archbishop, two bishops, eleven earls, fifteen barons and 300 knights – killed at the disastrous battle of Flodden.

The Scottish monarch had embarked on the venture after Queen Anne of France, under the terms of the Auld Alliance between Scotland and her nation, appealed to him to 'break a lance' on her behalf and act as her chosen knight.

Crossing the border into England at the head of a 25,000-strong army that included 7,500 clansmen and their kinsmen, James engaged a 20,000-strong force commanded by the Earl of Surrey.

Despite their numerical superiority and bravery,

however, the Scots proved no match for the skilled English artillery and superior military tactics of Surrey.

Nearly 35 years later, in 1547, Sir James Forrester, 7th Chief of Clan Forrester, was on the field at the equally disastrous battle of Pinkie, near Musselburgh, on Scotland's east coast, following the invasion of a 25,000-strong English army under the Duke of Somerset.

An estimated 3,000 Scots, including Sir James Forrester, who fought under the leadership of the Earl of Argyll, were killed in the battle.

Although bearers of the Forrester name had proven loyal in their support of the Stuart monarchs, this support faltered after the accession to the throne of the ill-starred daughter of James V, Mary, Queen of Scots.

Along with a number of other Protestant nobles who included Patrick Ruthven, 3rd Lord Ruthven, the Forresters were implicated in the conspiracy to brutally kill the Queen's Italian private secretary and musician David Rizzio.

It was in March of 1566 that a party of heavily-armed conspirators entered Mary's private chambers in the Palace of Holyrood, at the foot of Edinburgh's Royal Mile, and stabbed Rizzio to death in full view of a horrified and seven-months pregnant Queen.

The Forresters also took to the field of battle in opposition to the ill-fated Queen at the battle of Langside in May of 1568.

She had earlier escaped from Lochleven Castle, in which she had been imprisoned after being forced to sign her abdication, by a body known as the Confederate Lords.

A group of nine earls, nine bishops, 18 lairds and others signed a bond declaring their support for her, and both sides met at Langside, near Glasgow.

Mary's forces, under the command of the Earl of Argyll, had been en route to the mighty bastion of Dumbarton Castle, atop its near inaccessible eminence on Dumbarton Rock, on the Clyde, when it was intercepted by a numerically inferior but tactically superior force led by her half-brother, the Earl of Moray.

Cannon fire had been exchanged between both sides before a force of Argyll's infantry tried to force a passage through to the village of Langside, but they were fired on by a disciplined body of musketeers and forced to retreat as Moray launched a cavalry charge on their confused ranks.

The battle proved disastrous for Mary and signalled the death knell of her cause, with more than 100 of her supporters killed or captured and Mary forced to flee into what she then naively thought would be the protection of her cousin, England's Queen Elizabeth – only to be executed on her orders nineteen years later.

Returning to their allegiance to the Stuart cause, the Forresters fought in support of Charles I and his successor Charles II during the bitter seventeenth century wars between King and Covenant.

By the early eighteenth century, however, bearers of the Forrester name were prominent in their support of what had become, following the Act of Union between Scotland and England in 1707, the British cause.

Colonel George Forrester, 5th Lord Forrester of Corstorphine, fought with distinction with the Grenadier and Life Guards during the wars of the Spanish Succession against France.

He was on the field of battle in 1708 at Oudenarde, Flanders, and a year later at Malplaquet – while he was wounded at the battle of Preston during the abortive Jacobite Rising of 1715.

Chapter four:

On the world stage

Far from the field of battle, bearers of the Forrester name and its equally popular spelling variations that include Forrest, Forester, Forster and Foster, have gained international acclaim.

Born in 1921, **Caye Forrester** was the American film and television actress whose film credits include the 1950 *DOA*.

The actress, who died in 2005, is also noted for both writing and co-starring in the 1961 thriller *Door-to-Door Maniac*, which also featured a screen appearance by country singer Johnny Cash.

A multi-award winning actress, producer and director, **Jodie Foster** was born Alicia Christian Foster in 1962 in Los Angeles.

Beginning her career at the tender age of three in television commercials, her first major film role came only ten years later in the 1976 *Taxi Driver*, and for which she received an Academy Award nomination for Best Supporting Actress.

An Academy Award for Best Actress came in 1989 for her role in *The Accused*, while two years later she won another Academy Award for Best Actress for her role as FBI agent Clarice Starling in *The Silence of the Lambs*.

Other popular films include *Nell*, from 1994, and the 2011 *Carnage*, for which she received a Golden Globe nomination for Best Actress in a Musical or Comedy.

Fluent in French and having dubbed herself in some French language versions of her films, she also holds a degree in literature from Yale University.

It later transpired that during her time at Yale she had been stalked by John Hinckley, Jr. – the gunman who attempted to assassinate U.S. President Ronald Regan in March of 1981.

Hinckley claimed his motive had been to impress the unsuspecting actress.

Best known for his role as a Dutch detective in the British television drama series *Van der Valk*, which ran for five series from 1972, **Barry Foster** was the film and television actor born in 1927 in Beeston, Nottinghamshire, and who died in 2002.

Trained as an actor at the Central School of Speech and Drama, London, his film credits include the 1956 *The Battle of the River Plate*, the 1966 *The Family Way*, and, from 1970, *Ryan's Daughter*.

Born William Forrest Andrews in Huntsville, Texas, in 1924, **Steve Forrest**, a younger brother of the American actress Dana Andrews, is the film and television actor whose screen credits include the 1962 *The Longest Day* and whose television credits from the 1960s include *Rawhide*, *The Fugitive* and *The Baron*.

The presenter of former British television shows that include *Tomorrow's World, Robot Wars* and *The Heaven and Earth Show*, **Phillipa Forrester** is the radio and television presenter, producer and author born in 1968 in Winchester, Hampshire.

Now a maker of wildlife films such as the *Halcyon River Diaries* series for the BBC, along with her husband the wildlife cameraman and producer Charlie Hamilton James, she is also the author of the 2004 *The River*.

In the world of music, **Maureen Forrester** was the renowned Canadian operatic contralto, born in 1930 in Montreal, of mixed Scots and Irish descent.

Singing in church and radio choirs from the age of 13 and later paying for voice lessons from her salary as a secretary for a telephone company, by 1956 she was in popular demand and touring extensively.

Married to the Canadian violinist and conductor Eugene Kash, her many acclaimed performances include singing Cordelia in 1966 in Handel's *Guilo Cesare*.

Made a Companion of the Order of Canada in 1967 and receiving a star on Canada's Walk of Fame in Toronto in 2000, the singer, who was the mother of the actors Linda and David Kash, died in 2010.

Recognised as the 'Father of American music', **Stephen Foster** was the great American songwriter of the nineteenth century whose many compositions remain popular to this day.

Born in 1826 in Lawrenceville, Pennsylvania, he later moved to Cincinnati, Ohio, to work as a book keeper in his brother's steamship company.

He had no formal musical training, but nevertheless penned memorable songs that include *Beautiful Dreamer*, *Camptown Races*, and *Old Folks at Home* (also known as *Swanee River*).

His *Jeanie with the Light Brown Hair* was inspired by his wife, while *Oh! Susanna* became the 'anthem' of the California Gold Rush of 1848 to 1855 and *Old Kentucky Home* is now the official song of the State of Kentucky.

Despite the immense popularity of his songs

in his lifetime, Foster did not earn much from them because of the limited nature at the time of legislation governing copyright and royalties.

Most of the profits went to sheet music publishers and printers, with *Oh! Susanna*, for example, earning him only $100.

By 1860 his fortunes had gone into decline, with his wife and daughter having left him, and he died only four years later at the age of 37.

All that was found in his battered old wallet were a few coins and a scrap of paper that simply said: *"Dear friends and gentle hearts"* – the title perhaps, of a song in the early stages of composition.

Inducted into the Songwriters Hall of Fame in 1970 and the Nashville Songwriters Hall of Fame in 2010, he is also honoured through January 13th, the date of his birth, recognised by United States National Observance as Stephen Foster Memorial Day.

Not only a musician, but also a poet, novelist and lecturer in law, **Gary Forrester** was born in 1946 in Decatur, Illinois, the son of an Irish-American basketball and baseball coach.

Having also lived in New Zealand and Australia, his best-selling albums of bluegrass music, under what he calls his 'nom de guitar' of Eddie Rambeaux, include the 1987 *Dust on the Bible* and his 1990 *Kamara*.

As a lawyer, he has represented the interest of Native North American tribes, while the title of his 2011 memoir, *Hunter, Blaw Thy Horn*, is the motto of Clan Forrester.

Born in 1919 in Hoylake, Merseyside, **Helen Forrester** was the pen-name of the Anglo-Canadian author Helen June Bhatia (neé Huband).

Settling in Edmonton, Alberta, where she married the noted Canadian theoretical physicist Avadh Bhatia, she wrote a series of novels based on memories of her native Merseyside.

These include her 1974 *Twopence to Cross the Mersey* and her 2003 *A Cuppa Tea and an Aspirin*.

The recipient of honorary doctorates from the University of Liverpool and the University of Alberta, she died in 2011.

Born Edwin Morgan Foster in 1879 in Marleybone, London, **E.M. Forster** was the English novelist and essayist whose works include *A Room with a View*, published in 1908 and adapted for the screen in 1985, and his 1924 *A Passage to India*, adapted for film in 1984.

He died in 1970, a year after being made a member of the Order of Merit.

Born in Paris in 1925, **Viviane Forrester** is the novelist, essayist and literary critic whose books include a 2009 biography of Virginia Woolf.

Best known for his *Horatio Hornblower* series of naval warfare novels, Louis Troughton Smith was better known by his pen-name of **C.S. Forester**.

Born in Cairo in 1899, his novels *A Ship of the Line* and *Flying Colours* were jointly awarded the 1938 James Tait Black Memorial Prize for fiction, while his 1935 *The African Queen* – not part of the 11-part *Hornblower* series – was filmed in 1951 starring Katherine Hepburn and Humphrey Bogart.

Later settling in Berkeley, California, he died in 1966.

He was the father of the Anglo-American industrial engineer and cycling activist **John Forrester**, born in 1929 in Dulwich, London.

Known as the 'Father of vehicular cycling', he is recognised as having been an early advocate of the provision of cycle lanes in towns and cities.

On the athletics field, **Stephanie Forrester**, born in 1969, is the English triathlon athlete who competed in 2000 at the first ever Olympic triathlon event, while on the rugby pitch **James Forrester**, born in Oxford in 1981, is the former English rugby union player who played for Gloucester Rugby and his national team.

In the much less physically demanding game of bridge, **Tony Forrester**, born in 1953, is both a British and World International Master, and, from 1993, bridge columnist for the *Sunday Telegraph* newspaper.

A pioneering American computer engineer and systems analyst, **Jay Wright Forrester** was born on a ranch in Anselmo, Nebraska, in 1918.

The ranch was first supplied with electric power while Forrester was in high school – after he built a wind-driven electrical system using old vehicle parts.

Studying electrical engineering at the University of Nebraska and later at Massachusetts Institute of Technology (MIT), during the Second World War he developed servo-mechanisms for gun mounts and the control of radar antenna.

Developer of what is known as the 'whirlwind' computer, he was also a pioneering founder of system dynamics.

Inducted into the Operational Research Hall of Fame in 2006, he is also a recipient of America's National Medal of Technology.

Born in 1949, **John Forrester** is the English historian of philosophy, science and medicine recognised as a leading expert on the history of psychoanalysis and the life and work of Sigmund Freud.

It is not only with their feet firmly rooted on the ground that bearers of the Forrester name have gained distinction.

Taking to the heavens, **Patrick G. Forrester**, born in 1957 in El Paso, Texas, is the retired U.S. Army colonel and NASA astronaut who logged more than 620 hours in space and undertook five space walks.

A recipient of the NASA Space Flight Medal, other awards include the Army Commendation Medal and the Defense Superior Service Medal.